Plays for Assembly and PSE

FEELINGS

Gordon Aspland

SOUTHGATE

First published 1999 by Southgate Publishers Ltd

Southgate Publishers Ltd
15 Barnfield Avenue
Exmouth
Devon EX8 2QE

Printed and bound in Great Britain by Bell & Bain Ltd, Glasgow.

British Library Cataloguing in Publication Data.
A CIP catalogue record for this book is available from the British Library.

ISBN 1–85741–039–4

CONTENTS

INTRODUCTION 4

TEACHER'S NOTES: 5

Play 1
THE ICE BLUE PORSCHE 7
✤ jumping to the wrong conclusions

Play 2
THE LAMB 13
✤ looking after our environment

Play 3
THE MOUNTAIN BIKE 18
✤ being self-centred

Play 4
JOEY AND FLO 23
✤ facing up to responsibility

Play 5
THE NEW COAT 28
✤ respect for other people's property

INTRODUCTION

This book of short plays comes after the success of the four books of short stories published so far: *Feelings*, *Choices*, *Situations* and *Starting Out*. The stories have had a number of uses including whole school and class assemblies, story writing in Language work and Personal and Social Education (PSE). The development of the Literacy Hour has meant that there is a need for suitable material for group reading by the children themselves. '*Plays for PSE*' has been written with this in mind, both providing group reading texts for the Literacy Hour and fulfilling the needs of PSE for children to be more pro-active in looking at their behaviour towards other people.

The plays can stand alone or be used after reading the appropriate story from the original book. The latter use helps the children to get very quickly into the pace and style of the play. The plays should take no more than ten minutes to read. I found that children need to read them twice, the first time to get a feel for the language and the second time to read with expression. I have given some readers two characters. This is because I have kept to a format of groups of five readers but in some stories I have needed more than five characters in order to keep the plot flowing. Some of these characters only have a few lines, so it is important for a reader to have two characters who appear at different times in a play, in order to feel a part of the play all the way through.

I have introduced an element of reading ability in the plays so that children of differing abilities can join together, something that does not happen too often in the Literacy Hour but is important in PSE. It is a very crude ability range based on sentence structure and vocabulary:

- ✤ reading age of about 6/7years
- ✤✤ reading age of about 8/9 years
- ✤✤✤ reading age of about 10/11+

The plays could be used purely as a Literacy Hour group reading session or within an extended PSE lesson using the discussion points and further activity. The plays could be acted out for the rest of the class or in a school assembly.

G. Aspland

TEACHER'S NOTES

PLAY 1: THE ICE-BLUE PORSCHE

Characters	*Reading Ability*	*Characters*	*Reading Ability*
Narrator	✤✤✤	Philip	✤
Tom	✤✤	Mrs Jones/ Tom's Mother	✤
Calvin	✤✤		

GROUP DISCUSSION:

How do you think Tom feels now?
What do you think he should do ?
In what ways was Tom kind to Calvin in the beginning?

ACTIVITY:

Finish the play, showing how Tom sorts out his problem. What do you think Calvin's reaction will be?

PLAY 2: THE LAMB

Characters	*Reading Ability*	*Characters*	*Reading Ability*
Narrator	✤✤✤	Calvin/ Mr Marks	✤✤
Lisa	✤✤	Tom	✤
Lakshmi/ Mrs Jones	✤✤		

GROUP DISCUSSION:

Why can't you keep a lamb as a pet at home?
How did the crisp packet get into the lambs' field?
Why did the lamb try to eat it?
How do you think Mr Marks feels?

ACTIVITY:

Make a list of all the things you must remember to do in order to keep yourselves and the animals safe when you visit a farm.

PLAY 3: THE MOUNTAIN BIKE

Characters	*Reading Ability*
Narrator	✤✤✤
Tom	✤✤
Calvin	✤
Mother/Robert	✤✤
Shop Assistant/Philip	✤

GROUP DISCUSSION:

Why was Calvin so upset when he heard about the grandfather clock?
How did Tom and Philip show their friendship to Calvin?
Why do you think Robert hasn't got any friends?

ACTIVITY:
At the end of the play Calvin's mother asked why the boys had his bicycle. Write an ending to the play showing how the boys explained why they had Calvin's bike.

PLAY 4: JOEY AND FLO

Characters	Reading Ability
Narrator/Mrs Jones	✤✤✤
Tom	✤✤
Joanne	✤✤
Subatra/Lisa	✤✤
Calvin/Mr Bell	✤

GROUP DISCUSSION:
Was it fair to blame Lisa because the guinea pigs escaped?
What happened because the boys didn't fulfil their responsibilities?
What are the responsibilities of looking after a pet?

ACTIVITY:
Find out what kind of pets the children in your class have. How are you going to show your results?

PLAY 5: THE NEW COAT

Characters	Reading Ability
Narrator/Philip	✤✤✤
Joanne	✤✤
Subatra	✤✤
Mother/Mrs Jones	✤
Father/Tom	✤

GROUP DISCUSSION:
How did Tom show a lack of respect for someone else's property?
What were Joanne's feelings when she saw the coat lying on the ground?
Did Joanne look after her coat properly?

Whose fault was it?
Joanne's parents for letting her take her coat to school?
Philip for suggesting to Tom to take the coat?
Tom for taking the coat and kicking it?
Joanne for leaving it on the bench?
Subatra for encouraging Joanne to play netball?

ACTIVITY:
Write a prayer about how we should show respect for other people's property.

Play 1

THE ICE-BLUE PORSCHE

CHARACTERS

Narrator
Calvin
Mrs Jones/Tom's Mother
Tom
Philip

SETTING

The children are busy working in the classroom. Mrs Jones brings a new boy into the classroom. His name is Calvin.

Mrs Jones: Class, this is Calvin. He's new to our school. I hope you'll make him feel welcome. I think you can sit beside Tom.

(*Calvin sits beside Tom*)

Tom: Hi, I'm Tom. Do you like football?

Calvin: Yeah, I was in the school team at my last school.

Tom: No kidding, what position did you play?

Calvin: Centre forward.

Philip: Do you play chess?

Mrs Jones: Now class, I want you to get your English exercise books out.

Tom: (*putting his hand up*) Please Miss, Calvin hasn't got a book.

Mrs Jones: Thank you, Tom. I'll sort him out in a minute. I'd like you all to finish the poem you started yesterday afternoon.

Narrator: Once Calvin knew what he had to write he noticed that the other children were using biros or pens.

Calvin: Please Miss, can I use this fountain pen?

Mrs Jones: Yes, of course you can. If you need any ink, just ask me.

Narrator: Calvin got out his pen. It was a gold and blue coloured fountain pen.

Tom: That's a nice pen.

Calvin: It was a present from my grandmother. It used to belong to my grandfather.

Philip: Why did she give it to you?

Calvin: When Grandpa died Grandma gave it to me as something to remember him by. Grandpa and Grandma used to live in Jamaica and my Grandpa worked for a very rich man. When they emigrated to Britain the rich man gave it to him as a goodbye present.

Philip: I had a nice pen once but my sister broke it.

Calvin: I love using this because it writes really well.

Narrator: The boys carried on with their work. Tom wrote with his old biro and Calvin wrote with his gold and blue fountain pen. The boys quickly became friends. They worked together in the classroom and played football at playtime. It was soon the end of the week.

Tom: Would like to come over to my house tomorrow to play?

Calvin: That'd be great. I must check with my mum tonight but I think it'll be all right. I'll phone you tonight.

Narrator: The next day Calvin arrived at Tom's house.

Tom's Mother: You must be Calvin, Tom told me you were coming over today. I'm Tom's mother if you haven't guessed by now.

Tom: You found the house all right. Come on upstairs.

Narrator: When Tom showed Calvin into his bedroom Calvin stood still, looking around.

Calvin: Where did you get all those cars from?

Tom: Collecting cars is my hobby. Come on, let's set up some ramps and play with them.

Calvin: This is a nice one.

Tom: That's my favourite car. It's a Porsche. I got it last Christmas.

Calvin: Can I play with it?

Tom: Well ... I suppose so. I don't usually play with it too much, I keep it for show. But if you're careful you can play with it.

Calvin: Gee, thanks, I'll be extra careful with it.

Narrator: The boys played for a couple of hours, zooming the cars up roads, under tunnels and over ramps.

Tom's Mother: (*calling from downstairs*) Boys, I have some tea for you.

Tom: Good, I'm hungry. We can watch TV while we eat.

Calvin: I can only stay for another half hour, then I'll have to go.

Narrator: The boys hungrily ate some sandwiches and then Calvin got ready to go.

Calvin: Thank you very much for the tea. I really enjoyed myself.

Tom's Mother: That's all right, it's been nice having you.

Calvin: Bye, Tom, see you on Monday.

Tom: Thanks for coming over, it's been great.

Narrator: Calvin left and Tom slumped into a chair to watch TV.

Tom's Mother: Now young man, I think a bit of a tidy up is in order.

Tom: I'll do it later.

Tom's Mother: Upstairs now!

Narrator: Tom went upstairs to tidy his room. He put all his cars away and then found an empty box. It was the box for his favourite Porsche.

Tom: I wonder where the Porsche is?

Narrator: Tom looked everywhere but he couldn't find the car.

Tom: Calvin must have taken it! What a rotten thing to do. I knew I shouldn't let him play with it. Some friend he's turned out to be. I'll sort him out on Monday!

✣ ✣ ✣ ✣ ✣

Narrator: On Monday morning Tom was determined to get his revenge on Calvin. Tom started to kick a ball around with Philip.

Calvin: Hi Tom, can I play too?

Tom: I don't want to play with you again! I know what you did and you're a cheating thief.

Calvin: What? I don't know what you're talking about.

Philip: What's going on? Why can't Calvin play?

Tom: He stole something from me when I thought he was my friend.

Philip: That's a bit rotten. Come on, we don't play with thieves.

Narrator: The boys left Calvin on his own. He really didn't know what to say. During the day they ignored him and refused to play with him during playtime.

Tom: I know how to get even with Calvin. I'll take that precious pen of his. Then he'll know what it's like to have something stolen from him.

Philip: Are you sure he stole your car?

Tom: I know he took it. He was playing with it all afternoon then it was missing. So I'm going to take his pen.

Philip: When will you take it?

Tom: You watch out for him at afternoon break. I'll sneak in and take it from his tray.

Narrator: And that's what Tom did. At the end of the day Calvin went to his tray but his pen was not there.

Calvin: Mrs Jones, I can't find my pen. I know I put it back before afternoon playtime.

Mrs Jones: Take all of your things out, it must be there.

Calvin: But I haven't got much in my tray, I know it isn't there. (*he starts to cry*)

Mrs Jones: This is what we'll do. Most of the others have gone now so tomorrow I'll get everyone to have a good look round. I am sure we'll find it.

Calvin: I hope we do. I'll be in real trouble if I've lost it. Do you think somebody has stolen it?

Mrs Jones: I can't think who'd do such a thing. I'm sure we'll find it tomorrow.

Narrator: Calvin went home sad and worried that day. Meanwhile the pen was in Tom's bag and he was beginning to wish he hadn't taken it.

Tom: What should I do with this pen?

Philip: Look, there's a drain. Why don't you drop the pen down it?

Narrator: Tom took the pen out of his bag and looked down at the drain. He quickly bent down, checked that nobody was watching him and dropped the pen through the bars of the cover. He heard Calvin's pen plop into the water.

Tom: There, now that thief Calvin will know what it's like to lose something for ever. Do you want to come to my house and play?

Philip: I've got to go home. I'm going shopping with my mum.

Narrator: Tom continued to walk home. When he opened his front door he was greeted by his mother.

Tom's Mother: You're getting careless with your things.

Tom: What do you mean?

Tom's Mother: Look what I found in the corner under the bed.

Narrator: There, sitting on the kitchen table, was his ice-blue Porsche!

Play 2

THE LAMB

CHARACTERS

Narrator
Tom
Lakshmi/Mrs Jones
Lisa
Calvin/Mr Marks

SETTING

The children are on a bus going to a farm for a class outing. None of them has ever been to a farm before.

Tom: The bus is slowing down. Are we nearly there?

Mrs Jones: Yes, I think the farm is just round the corner.

Narrator: The children looked excitedly out of the windows of the coach as it pulled into the farmyard. As they got out of the coach they were greeted by a strong farmyard smell.

Calvin: What a pong! I'm not going to let go of my nose until we leave.

Tom: How are you going to eat your lunch and breathe at the same time?

Lisa: Do all farms smell like this? It's horrible, I'd rather be in the city smelling cars.

Mrs Jones: Don't be silly, you'll soon get used to it. At least the smell won't hurt you, not like car fumes. Here comes the farmer, Mr Marks.

Mr Marks: Good morning everybody. I hope you had a safe trip here. Welcome to Highfield Farm. I am going to tell you all about the farm first.

Narrator: The children listened as Mr Marks told them about the herd of milking cows, flocks of sheep and fields of wheat.

Mr Marks: Half of you go with your teacher to see the combine harvester. The rest can come with me to see the cows being milked. When we meet back at the pens there be a surprise for you.

Tom: What's the surprise?

Mr Marks: If I told you it wouldn't be a surprise.

Narrator: Tom, Lakshmi and Lisa went with Mr Marks to the milking parlour. They saw the herd waiting to go to be milked.

Mr Marks: Mind where you step. I see some of you didn't bring boots.

Tom: Oh no, it's too late! I've just trodden in that big cow pat!

Lakshmi: Your new white trainers aren't very white any more!

Mr Marks: Never mind, I'll get the hose out. You can wash your shoes before you go home.

Lakshmi: Do you milk the cows by hand or do you use machines?

Mr Marks: We milk all the cows by these machines.

Lisa: It's noisy in here. Look, the cows don't mind when the machines squeeze the milk out.

Tom: I can see milk going into that glass thing.

Lakshmi: Can we have a drink of the milk?

Mr Marks: No, this milk has to go to the dairy first. By tomorrow it'll be in bottles and on your breakfast table. I think it's time for your surprise. Follow me.

Narrator: The children met up with the other group and waited to see what was going to happen. Mr Marks gave out a number of baby bottles of milk.

Lisa: This bottle isn't for me, is it?

Tom: We're not babies!

Lakshmi: Don't be silly, I think we're going to feed the lambs, aren't we?

Mr Marks: She's quite right. Hold the bottles down and hold on tight.

Narrator: Mr Marks opened a large door and several lambs came running out, looking desperately for their feed. They ran up to the bottles and everyone started shouting and laughing as milk sprayed everywhere.

Tom: I can feel this one sucking at the bottle. He must be hungry.

Lisa: Look at his little black face, I wish I could take him home with me.

Lakshmi: The milk has dripped all over my skirt.

Tom: My bottle's empty already. The lamb's trying to suck my fingers now!

Lisa: Do people have lambs as pets, you know, like a dog or a cat?

Lakshmi: It would have to stay in a field. It would be a bit smelly in the house.

Narrator: Once the bottles were empty the lambs were gathered together and put into a field. The children washed their hands and then had their own lunch.

Calvin: That was a great morning. I loved feeding the lambs.

Lisa: I hope we can see them once more before we go.

Lakshmi: You'd put one in your bag and take it home if you could.

Tom: We'd better search your bag before we go.

Lisa: Don't worry, I don't think my parents would let me have a pet lamb at our house.

Narrator: The children were sitting at a picnic table eating their lunch. When they had finished they wandered over to sketch some of the farm buildings and machinery. They didn't see the crisp packet left under the table. The wind picked it up and blew it over towards the lambs' field.

Mrs Jones: Well children, are you enjoying your day?

Calvin: It's been great. I'm even getting used to the smell.

Lisa: I loved the lambs best. Can we go and see them again before we leave?

Mrs Jones: I'm sure we can have one last look, but you must finish your pictures first.

Tom: Can we feed them again? I can still feel the lamb's little hot mouth sucking on my fingers.

Mrs Jones: I think their next feed is later in the day when we have gone home.

Calvin: What a pity. That was my favourite thing.

Narrator: The children finished their pictures and began to gather at the gate to the field to have one last look at the lambs.

Lisa: I think they're lovely. Where's the black-faced one that I was feeding?

Tom: I think it's that one lying down over there.

Lisa: All the other ones are playing. Why is that one lying down?

Lakshmi: I think it's sick. It's trying to get up but it can't.

Tom: It looks as if it can't breathe.

Lisa: Quickly, we must get Mr Marks.

Narrator: Lisa and Tom ran to find Mr Marks. He climbed over the fence and ran to the sick lamb. He examined it carefully and then looked down its throat. He pulled something out. The lamb gave a snort, jumped up and ran off.

Tom: Look, the lamb's up. I think he's better now.

Lisa: Thank goodness for that. I couldn't have gone home not knowing what was going to happen.

Lakshmi: Here's Mr Marks. What was wrong with the lamb?

Narrator: Mr Marks' face was very stern. The children stopped smiling.

Mr Marks: I found this crisp packet in the lamb's throat. It nearly died. Now who can tell me how it got there?

Play 3

THE MOUNTAIN BIKE

CHARACTERS

Narrator
Tom
Philip
Robert
Calvin
Shop Assistant
Mother

SETTING

It is nearly Calvin's birthday and he and Tom are in a shop looking at mountain bicycles. Tom is looking closely at a bright yellow bicycle.

Tom: That one's exactly the same as mine. It's got eighteen gears.

Calvin: Did your parents really pay £250 for it?

Tom: They gave it to me for my birthday and Christmas. I saved some of my pocket money as well.

Calvin: I'd love to have a bike like that. I wonder if my mum will get it for me for my birthday if I ask her?

Shop Assistant: Can I help you two?

Tom: We're just having a look. Can we have a brochure for these bikes, please? Have you got bikes like that one in other colours?

Shop Assistant: Just wait there and I will get you a brochure. I'm afraid we don't have any green or blue bikes left.

Calvin: Thank you, but I think I like the yellow one best anyway.

Shop Assistant: Here you are. The prices are on the back.

Narrator: When Calvin got home he read the brochure eagerly. When his mother got back from work he ran up to her waving the page showing the bright yellow mountain bicycle.

Calvin: Look, Mum, I've seen what I want for my birthday.

Mother: It certainly looks very nice but look at the price! I couldn't afford one of those. You know we don't have much money, Calvin.

Calvin: But, Mum, it's what I really want.

Mother: That bicycle would cost a whole month's wages. I'm sorry Calvin, it's impossible.

Narrator: Calvin was so disappointed he ran to his bedroom in floods of tears. When he heard the grandfather clock strike six he went sadly downstairs for his tea. No one talked about the mountain bike.

✤ ✤ ✤ ✤ ✤

Narrator: The next day Tom wanted to know what Calvin's mother had said.

Tom: Are you going to get a bike for your birthday, Calvin?

Calvin: Mum said she couldn't afford it. But my birthday is next week and she hasn't asked me yet for any other ideas.

Tom: I reckon she's going to surprise you with it.

Calvin: Do you think so? Do you think she'll get the yellow one? I'd really love that one.

Narrator: The morning of Calvin's birthday came. He looked at the end of his bed and saw a square box. He felt disappointed when he began to open it but he cheered up when he saw what was inside.

Calvin: Wow, it's a bicycle helmet! That must mean that I've got the bike as well!

Narrator: Calvin raced downstairs to look for his bike. Then he saw it. It was an old drop-handled, racing bicycle.

Calvin: *(to himself)* What's that? It's not yellow, it's not new, it's not even a mountain bike!

Mother: I hope you like it, love. I knew that all you wanted was a bicycle and this was all the man at the shop had in my price range. It's in very good condition for its age. It's got ten gears you know.

Narrator: Calvin didn't know what to say. He tried to look pleased. Later that day he decided to take his bicycle for a ride to the local rec. After all, he decided, it might not be as bad as it looked.

Tom: Is that your new bike?

Philip: It looks a fast bike.

Calvin: It's not quite what I wanted but it goes all right.

Philip: I used to have one like that. It was a blue one. I have this mountain bike now.

Robert: Nobody has a bike like that now. It's rubbish, this is the best one you can get. You can go anywhere on this.

Calvin: You can on this one too!

Tom: Come on Cal, don't listen to him, he's just trying to wind you up.

Philip: Racing bikes can really go fast, you know.

Robert: You can't go fast over rough ground, not like riding a mountain bike. You won't be able to catch me on your old Droopy-bars. Come on, follow me.

Philip: Wait for us.

Narrator: The boys chased after Robert but Calvin struggled to keep up on his old racing bicycle.

Robert: Come on Droopy-bars, can't you keep up?

Tom: Slow down, Robert, he can't go as fast as you.

Robert: He shouldn't have such a rubbish bike.

Philip: It's too bumpy for his old bike.

Robert: Hurry up, Droopy-bars, is the ground too rough for you?

Narrator: Just then the thin wheels of Calvin's racing bike hit a hole in the ground. His wheel buckled and he went flying off his bicycle.

Tom: Are you all right, Cal?

Philip: Oh no, look at your front wheel!

Robert: I told you that bike was rubbish.

Philip: Leave him alone.

Robert: You need to get a decent bike like this. I'm going now. See you tomorrow.

Tom: Ignore him, he's just big-headed.

Calvin: He's right, this bike is rubbish, I hate it!

Narrator: Calvin threw his mangled bike onto the ground and ran home. Sometime later he realised what he had done and wondered what he was going to tell his mum.

Mother: Hello, did you have a nice ride on your bicycle?

Calvin: It was all right. Where's the grandfather clock?

Mother: Well, I didn't have enough money to pay for your bicycle and a helmet so I sold the clock.

Calvin: But we've always had that clock, Mum. It was your favourite thing in the house.

Mother: Yes, it was the most valuable thing we had.

Calvin: Why did you sell it?

Mother: You were so keen to have a bicycle and I didn't want to let you down. Why are you crying, Calvin?

Narrator: Just then the doorbell rang. Calvin opened the door and there were Tom and Philip with his bicycle. It looked perfect.

Tom: Hi Cal, we didn't know what to get you for your birthday so we took your bike to the shop and had your wheel repaired.

Philip: It's as good as new. Do you want to come and try it out?

Mother: Hello boys, why have you got Calvin's bicycle?

Play 4

JOEY AND FLO

CHARACTERS

Narrator/Mrs Jones
Tom
Calvin/Mr Bell
Joanne
Subatra/Lisa

SETTING

Mrs Jones has brought her guinea pigs into school for the children to look after. She has put them on a table in the classroom.

Mrs Jones: Does anybody know what guinea pigs eat?

Subatra: Lots of green food, like lettuce and dandelion leaves.

Mrs Jones: Yes, that's right, what else do they like?

Calvin: Do they like carrots?

Tom: Do they like potatoes, not chips but you know, raw potatoes?

Mrs Jones: Carrots are very good for them but not potatoes and especially not chips!

Joanne: Oh look, Joey's done a wee on Calvin's Maths book!

Calvin: Good, I don't like Maths.

Mrs Jones: I think we can find you a new Maths book, Calvin.

Tom: Who's going to look after them while they're in the classroom?

Subatra: Maybe we could have a rota.

Mrs Jones: That's a good idea. But don't forget that that means not only feeding them but also checking on their water, exercising them and, most important, cleaning their cage.

Joanne: Can Subatra and I be first?

Calvin: That's not fair. You are always first.

Tom: Calvin and I should be first because we haven't got a pet.

Subatra: Neither have I! You two wouldn't want to get your hands dirty cleaning the cage.

Calvin: We'd do a better job than you.

Mrs Jones: Stop arguing, I'll tell you what is going to happen. Tom and Calvin can look after them on Monday and Thursday, Subatra and Joanne on Tuesday and Wednesday. I think it's fair that you all clean the cage out on Friday.

Tom: Great, we can feed them today. Come on Cal, we can find some dandelion leaves.

Calvin: Okay. I'll check their water first.

Narrator: All went well until Thursday when the boys forgot it was their turn to look after Joey and Flo. They were playing football when Tom suddenly remembered.

Tom: Cal, we're supposed to be feeding the guinea pigs now.

Calvin: We're having a good game of football. Let's pretend that we forgot.

Tom: Do you think I should ask the girls if they'd like to look after Joey and Flo?

Calvin: Yes, that's a better idea.

Tom: Subatra, would you and Jo like to look after the guinea pigs today? Cal and I are in a good football game.

Subatra: Okay, we've got nothing to do.

Calvin: Thanks for doing it.

Joanne: You owe us for doing it. Come on Subatra, let's take the guinea pigs onto the field.

Subatra: Look, here comes Mr Bell, I wonder what he wants?

Mr Bell: You're just the two girls I want to see. Could you tidy the Music trolley, please?

Joanne: Yes, all right Sir. We'll go now.

Mr Bell: Thank you, girls.

Subatra: Why did you say that, Jo? We have to feed the guinea pigs!

Joanne: Well it's not really our turn, let the boys do it.

Subatra: I know, go and ask Lisa, she's not doing anything.

Joanne: Hello, Lisa, could you do us a favour?

Lisa: It depends on what it is.

Joanne: Could you feed Joey and Flo? It's really the boys' turn but they're playing football. We have to go in and help Mr Bell.

Lisa: But I'm allergic to the fur, it makes me sneeze.

Joanne: You don't have to touch them, just pick a few dandelion leaves and put them into the cage.

Lisa: Oh, all right.

Narrator: Lisa picked some dandelion leaves and took them to the cage. She really wanted to stroke the guinea pigs. In spite of her allergy she opened the cage door and began stroking Joey and Flo.

Lisa: Ahhhchoooo, Ahhhchoooo ... oh no, my allergy!

Narrator: Lisa ran off to get away from the guinea pigs. She forgot that she had left the door of the cage open. When next morning came the guinea pigs had disappeared. Mrs Jones was not happy.

Tom: Joanne and Subatra left the cage door open.

Calvin: They said they'd feed the guinea pigs.

Joanne: We didn't, we asked Lisa to feed the guinea pigs.

Lisa: I'm sorry. I started sneezing and then I forgot about the door.

Mrs Jones: You are the last person who should be blamed, Lisa. The others should have been looking after them!

Calvin: We'll start hunting for them.

Tom: I'll look behind the shed and swimming pool.

Joanne: Subatra and I'll search the field. They're probably hunting for dandelion leaves.

Narrator: The children looked all over the school. It was Mr Bell who found Joey. Unfortunately Joey had fallen into the school pond and drowned. There was no sign of Flo. All the children were very, very upset.

Tom: I think Flo might have gone into one of the gardens next to the school field.

Calvin: I'll ask if I can look in their gardens.

Mrs Jones: I think that's a very good idea.

Joanne: I hope that Flo hasn't been run over by a car.

Lisa: Or eaten by a cat.

Narrator: After the weekend the children were eager to find out if there was any news about Flo. Tom carried a box into the classroom.

Tom: Guess what everyone, I've found Flo.

Calvin: Where did you find her?

Lisa: Is she all right?

Tom: She's fine, but look at what has happened!

Joanne: She's had three little babies!

Tom: Yes, two females and one male.

Lisa: I think we should call the male guinea pig Joey.

Mrs Jones: I think that's an excellent idea, Lisa.

Play 5

THE NEW COAT

CHARACTERS

Narrator
Joanne
Mother/Mrs Jones
Philip
Subatra
Father/Tom

SETTING

Joanne's mother has ordered a new coat from her catalogue for Joanne. Joanne has rushed home from school.

Joanne: Hello Mum. Has it arrived yet?

Mother: Look on the kitchen table.

Narrator: Joanne ran into the kitchen. The parcel was on the table.

Joanne: Can I open it? I'll be careful not to damage the bag in case it needs to go back.

Mother: Of course you can.

Joanne: Mmmmm, it's a lovely warm coat, so nice and cosy.

Father: That's a nice coat. I like the green colour.

Mother: I think it's too pale. It will show the dirt.

Joanne: It's just the colour I wanted, nobody else has this colour. Can I wear it to school tomorrow?

Mother: No, I don't think that's a good idea.

Joanne: Oh, please! I'll look after it, I promise.

Mother: What do you think, dear?

Father: It cost a lot of money.

Joanne: I won't play netball or run around with it on. I promise.

Mother: All kinds of accidents could happen.

Father: Oh go on, let her wear it.

Mother: Okay, you can wear it to school.

Joanne: Oh thank you! I promise to look after it. I can't wait until tomorrow.

✤ ✤ ✤ ✤ ✤

Narrator: The next day Joanne was up early.

Mother: I wonder why you're up so soon!

Joanne: I thought I might go into school early.

Mother: You don't want to be too early. Nobody will be there to see you.

Joanne: I think the doorbell rang, I'll get it. Hello Subatra.

Subatra: Hi Jo, are you ready?

Joanne: Bye Mum, we're off.

Subatra: I like your new coat. Where did you get it?

Joanne: My mum ordered it from her catalogue. What do you think about the colour?

Subatra: It's nice, I like that shade of green.

Joanne: Mum thought it was too light but I think it's great.

Subatra: Yes, it's light but that colour's in now. Why didn't she like it?

Joanne: She said it would get too dirty. I had a really hard time getting her to let me wear it to school.

Subatra: How did you get her to say yes?

Joanne: I had to promise to look after it. Dad backed me up.

Subatra: There are the others. Come and show them your new coat.

Narrator: Joanne was quickly surrounded by admiring girls. Soon it was time to go to class, Joanne carefully put her coat onto her peg. At playtime she was careful not to run around and get knocked whilst wearing her new coat. By lunch time the sun was shining and it was very warm. The other girls asked her to play netball so she took off her coat and put it on a bench. The boys came out into the playground as well.

Tom: Come on Phil. Let's play football.

Philip: What are we going to use for goalposts?

Tom: Take your jumper off.

Philip: Okay, but we need more. How about that coat over there?

Tom: That green one? I'll go and get it.

Narrator: Tom got Joanne's coat and put it on the ground to act as a goalpost for their game of football. When Philip scored a goal, Tom was so annoyed he kicked the coat, leaving a huge dirty footprint on the pale green material.

Joanne: Ahhhhhhhh! What have you done?

Mrs Jones: What's the matter, Jo?

Subatra: Tom's ruined Jo's new coat.

Tom: I haven't. It's only a bit of dirt.

Joanne: But it's ruined. I told my mum that I'd look after it.

Mrs Jones: Why did you boys take it?

Tom: I was only borrowing it.

Philip: We were only using it for a goalpost.

Tom: I didn't mean to kick it.

Joanne: Why didn't you use your own coat?

Tom: We didn't bring our coats outside.

Philip: We were using our own jumpers.

Mrs Jones: Yes, but you shouldn't use other people's things without asking them first.

Philip: It was only for a few minutes.

Tom: It's only an old coat.

Joanne: It's not an old coat, you idiot.

Subatra: It's a brand new coat and Jo's going to be in real trouble because of you.

Narrator: Joanne was very upset and began to cry. Mrs Jones took the children to the office and made some telephone calls.

Mrs Jones: I've talked to your mother, Jo. She's coming to collect you.

Joanne: Is she very angry about the coat?

Mrs Jones: She knows that it was not really your fault. But I don't think she is happy. I've also talked to your parents, Tom.

Tom: What did they say?

Mrs Jones: You'll have to pay to have the coat cleaned.

Philip: I'll help pay as well.

Subatra: It serves you two right. I hope it costs a lot of money!

Narrator: Joanne's coat looked as good as new when it came back from the cleaners but it didn't really feel new any more. She didn't wear it to school again.